FASHION BUYER

By Jessica Cohn

Reading Consultant: Susan Nations, M.Ed.,
author/literacy coach/consultant in literacy development

Gareth Stevens
Publishing

Please visit our web site at **www.garethstevens.com.**
For a free catalog describing Gareth Stevens Publishing's list of high-quality books,
call 1-800-542-2595 (USA) or 1-800-387-3178 (Canada).
Gareth Stevens Publishing's fax: 1-877-542-2596

Library of Congress Cataloging-in-Publication Data
Cohn, Jessica.
    Fashion buyer / Jessica Cohn.
        p. cm. — (Cool careers : on the go)
    Includes bibliographical references and index.
    ISBN-10: 1-4339-0002-5   ISBN-13: 978-1-4339-0002-0 (lib. bdg.)
    ISBN-10: 1-4339-0166-8   ISBN-13: 978-1-4339-0166-9 (soft cover)
    1. Fashion merchandising—Vocational guidance—Juvenile literature. I. Title.
    literature. I. Title.
    HD9940.A2C57   2009
    746.9'2023—dc22   2008036433

This edition first published in 2009 by
Gareth Stevens Publishing
A Weekly Reader® Company
1 Reader's Digest Rd.
Pleasantville, NY 10570-7000 USA

Copyright © 2009 by Gareth Stevens, Inc.

Executive Managing Editor: Lisa M. Herrington
Creative Director: Lisa Donovan
Editor: Joann Jovinelly
Designer: Paula Jo Smith
Photo Researcher: Kimberly Babbitt
Publisher: Keith Garton

Picture credits: Cover and title page: Jose Luis Pelaez, Inc./Corbis; p. 5 AP Images/Dawn
Vilella; p. 6 AP Images/Stephen Chernin; p. 8 David P Hall/Corbis; p. 11 Eric Ryan/Getty
Images; p. 12 Courtesy of Dena Stokes; p. 13 RF/Alamy; p. 15 Dream Pictures/Corbis; p. 16
Iconica/Getty; p. 17 RF/Jupiter Images; p. 19 Bryan Bedder/Getty; p. 20 Corbis Sygma; p. 21
Christopher Peterson; p. 22 Simon Marcus/Corbis; p. 23 Stephen Lovekin/Getty Images;
p. 25 AP Images/Mary Altaffer; p. 26 TWPhoto/Corbis; p. 27 Everett Collection; p. 28 AP
Images/Rick Bowmer

Printed in the United States of America

1 2 3 4 5 6 7 8 9 10 09 08

CONTENTS

Words in the glossary appear in **bold** type the first time they are used in the text.

TM

CHAPTER 1

IT'S A BUYER'S WORLD

Look around any shopping mall in the United States. There are a lot of goods for shoppers to buy. Some stores sell clothes. Others sell home goods, such as pillows and linens. A few sell only **accessories**, like handbags and shoes. Fashion buyers fill each of those stores with items. They choose the clothing styles and colors. They decide what goods will end up on store shelves and in displays.

Following Trends

Fashion buyers make these choices carefully. They study sales reports to see what items are selling well. They also read fashion magazines, search the Internet, and watch TV to find out what celebrities are wearing. Buyers need to keep a sharp eye out for fashion **trends**. Those are styles that quickly become popular.

The Mall of America, in Bloomington, Minnesota, is filled with many goods thanks to fashion buyers.

Fashion buyers often travel to other countries. They attend fashion shows and **trade exhibitions** in major cities. They visit **showrooms** for ideas, too. The showrooms in New York City are especially famous. There, **designers** offer their new products.

Buyers quickly scoop up what they think will sell well. Understanding the history of fashion and watching people with style helps buyers decide what will become popular.

A Matter of Style

People who work as fashion buyers are often very stylish. Talented buyers understand and respect the role of fashion. Looking good can help people succeed. Fashion can be just plain fun, too!

Designers sell their designs to fashion buyers directly out of their showrooms.

Buying Time

8:00 A.M. Arrive at work. Swing by your assistant's desk. Ask for notes from the meeting with the handbag salesperson.

8:15 A.M. Examine sales reports and reorder most popular items.

9:15 A.M. Check fashion news online. Look at celebrity photos from a recent movie opening. Note one dress that is especially interesting. Ask your assistant to find out which designer made it.

9:30 A.M. Attend meeting. Bring draft of the new **budget**. Request more money to fill out the dress department.

12:00 P.M. Break for lunch. Eat at desk while preparing for next meeting. Ask your assistant to return invitations to two upcoming fashion shows and make necessary travel plans.

Taking Stock

To become a buyer, you need a clear understanding of clothing styles. You also need keen business skills. Buyers serve many different kinds of customers. They need a sharp sense of which styles will appeal to different people. Being successful requires careful planning. It also requires some risk-taking when spotting a trend that you think will sell well.

Where They Work

Fashion buyers work for large and small businesses all over the world. **Wholesale** buyers buy items from manufacturers. They then sell those items to stores and shopping web sites. **Retail** buyers purchase items

Can you picture yourself in fashion?

from wholesale buyers. Sometimes retail buyers get goods directly from a manufacturer before selling them to the public.

What They Do

Even if you love to shop, being a fashion buyer can be difficult. Your decisions must be clear and thoughtful. You need to know what people like. Successful buyers know what customers want right now and what they will want in the near future. You also must understand what shoppers will pay for products. To succeed, you need to build a positive track record. The items that you buy for stores must sell well.

Is Fashion Buying Right for You?

If you think you might like fashion buying, ask yourself these questions:

- Do you like to shop?
- Do you have a strong sense of style?
- Are you interested in business?
- Do you like to travel?
- Are you good at solving problems?
- Do you enjoy working with people?

If so, a career in fashion buying might be right for you!

CHAPTER 2

SHOPPING FOR A LIVING

Fashion buyers are constantly thinking about new trends. They read fashion magazines and visit web sites to see what styles and products are popular. They pay close attention to what people are wearing. Buyers shop showrooms and attend fashion shows, searching for looks that create excitement. Then buyers use those ideas to decide what to buy.

Often, ideas come to buyers from designers who seek them out. New designers typically send buyers a "one sheet." That is a sheet or a postcard that offers a quick look at their designs. Established designers usually send a full catalog. A designer's catalog features all the items in the season's collection.

The Future Is Now

To keep ideas flowing, buyers must think quickly. They need to recognize what items are not selling and figure out why. Sharp buyers can help stores cut their losses by spotting mistakes early.

Fashion shows help buyers make decisions.

Buyers must always focus on the future. They need to think about what clothing styles will be popular in upcoming seasons. Clothes that will be in stores in the fall are purchased at least six months earlier.

By the Numbers

When people think about fashion, many of them think of *haute couture*, or high fashion. They think about models and fancy stores in New York and Paris. Yet the number-one store in the United States in 2007 was Wal-Mart, the discount retail chain. The number-six store was Target, another discount retailer. Sears department store was number eight. (The other stores in the top 10 did not sell clothing.)

On the Job:
Fashion Buyer Dena Stokes

Dena Stokes is vice president of Macy's East and a fashion buyer for Macy's juniors' department.

Q: Why did you become a fashion buyer?

Stokes: I was working at a department store during my last semester of college and found that I liked what the retail buying office provided — a good balance of skills in a dynamic and people-oriented environment.

Q: What do you like most about your job?

Stokes: There is always a new challenge and a new opportunity for you when you walk in the door in the morning.

Q: What is difficult about fashion buying?

Stokes: Retail is an extremely fast-paced and competitive environment. [You must be able to handle the] factors that can affect your business: competitors lowering pricing, the economic environment, a sudden snowstorm — all of which affect sales results but are out of your immediate control.

Q: What is rewarding about this line of work?

Stokes: Seeing what you bought coming into a store and selling well! This direct connection from office actions to bottom line results is rare in the corporate world.

Q: What advice do you have for students who are thinking about a job as a fashion buyer?

Stokes: Retail buying is a great career that I have found to be very rewarding. I still like coming into work after almost 20 years in the business!

Working in fashion requires teamwork.

Building Relationships

Buyers build special relationships with their **suppliers**. Those are the people who sell them items. Some suppliers can fill an order in a few days. Others cannot send items as quickly. As a buyer, you need to know which suppliers are fast. You have to plan ahead, knowing when goods will be available.

As a buyer, you may also work with designers. There is usually a give and take of ideas. Buyers want to learn what excites designers, and designers want to know what fashions buyers want.

CHAPTER 3

IN FASHION

Some fashion buyers work for the world's top designers. Yet buying and designing are just part of the picture. Many other related careers are open to people who study fashion. Kim Agnew has worked for Ralph Lauren and Martha Stewart. Her job was deciding how certain products were presented to people. That is another way to go. What Agnew liked most about her job, she says, was working with talented people. "You really 'get' that anything is possible. [It's] a powerful lesson," she says. "It's the **collaboration**, the creativity, and the level of excellence that drive you."

If you enjoy being around interesting, artistic people, a career in fashion may sound like a dream. But success in the fashion business does not come easily. For every buyer who does well, at least six others fail. How can you ensure your success? Making a name for yourself in the fashion industry often starts with your training.

How to Become Successful

Often, the best fashion jobs go to people who work hard for them. Many budding fashion workers compete for a few top positions. Agnew studied

Some fashion buyers work for fabric stores. They look for the latest prints and colors.

art and history in college. She then worked to get an **internship**, or starter job, before graduating.

While in college or art school, up-and-coming fashion buyers take classes in fashion **merchandising**. Students also take classes in marketing and

advertising. They learn about art and business. Some students earn a bachelor's degree before applying to a training program with a retail store.

Fashion Skills Set

With training, students can go into merchandising or buying. They can also become **marketers**. Fashion merchandisers track fashion trends. Some merchandisers advise store department heads on how to best display merchandise. Other kinds of merchandisers do that work themselves. Fashion marketers promote clothing and designer brands to media professionals such as magazine editors. They often advertise goods, too.

Creative people who work in the fashion industry often share ideas.

Fashion merchandisers make clothing look good!

Fashion Merchandising

Merchandisers are interested in the business side of fashion. They might develop plans that let designers or stores better understand their shoppers. Merchandisers sometimes advise stores about ways

On the Job: Merchandising

Kim Agnew got started in fashion merchandising when she landed an internship. The firm she worked for was putting together a book about home design. That led to even better jobs, including leading the style team for Martha Stewart's TV shows. "Knowing how to reach the consumer — what moves and interests them — is the deal," Agnew says.

to create more interesting shopping experiences. That can include offering related goods in one department or offering to personalize goods. They may offer ideas about creating displays for product or clothing lines. They also advise designers or stores on fashion trends.

Fashion Marketing

Marketers get people excited about new products and clothing. Marketers are good at creating interest in products. To do their jobs, marketers develop advertising. They also create events, such as fashion shows, that get people talking. They can use their contacts in the fashion world to showcase their products.

On the Job: Fashion Marketing

Julie Lambert talks to media professionals about brands of clothing and jewelry. When she was marketing Cambio jeans, she sent a pair to TV talk show host Oprah Winfrey. After the jeans were featured as one of "Oprah's Favorite Things," a web site that sold them went from 400 hits a day to 60,000. "The buyers started wanting hundreds of pairs," Lambert says.

A fashion show is a way to market clothing to buyers and consumers.

Fashion Buying

As a buyer, you use fashion know-how and track trends to pick items you think people will buy. The merchandiser makes your clothing or home accessories look good. The marketer tells the media about your products. Large companies usually employ people who specialize in buying, merchandising, or marketing. Many small companies, though, do not hire different people to do those jobs. They need one person who can perform all those tasks. In cases such as this, a fashion buyer may also be responsible for tasks related to merchandising and marketing.

CHAPTER 4

BEYOND FASHION SCHOOL

Have you seen the movie or the Broadway show *Legally Blonde*? The main character in both is a young woman named Elle Woods. The viewer first meets her as she graduates fashion school. Next, she enters law school. The things she learned about fashion help her in her new role as a student lawyer.

The story hints that being smart about fashion can mean being smart about life. There is a lot more to being a buyer than just shopping, after all. You must plan

What can *you* do with a fashion degree?

ahead and then work through your plan. You must learn as much as you can before you make decisions. "In sales and in the buying end, you do a lot of [thinking]," says fashion marketer Julie Lambert.

No-Fear Career

Perhaps most important, you need to love fashion. You need to throw yourself into the job and be ready to learn from your mistakes. Tricia Smith is the national merchandise manager for Nordstrom department store. She told *Cosmo Girl* that buyers must study "everything

On the Job: Visual Merchandiser

Bergdorf Goodman is a luxury department store in New York City. Linda Fargo is Bergdorf's senior vice president of visual merchandising and store presentation. She is also its women's fashion director. Fargo is in charge of the store's design, its displays, and the fashions sold there. She says much of her success comes from putting customers' needs first. When working in fashion, "you have to be careful not to shop with yourself in mind," she told *New York Magazine*.

from pop culture to runway shows, magazines, and celebrities — because everything influences the customer." Jen Rue, of the web site rue21, added, "Be prepared to think on your feet . . . and make mistakes! Not everything you buy is going to sell."

Getting Personal

Fashion careers can take many twists and turns. They can involve a lot of travel, too. People may like different work roles at different stages in life.

Some people take what they've learned and go out on their own. They can work as **consultants** to businesses or individuals. Consultants use their talent and experience to help the people who hire them.

Some fashion buyers find success as personal shoppers. They work for people who need to look good but do not have the time or know-how to do it alone. Sometimes business people hire personal shoppers to select clothing that improves their appearance. Many celebrities hire personal shoppers, too.

A career in fashion can take you places!

On the Job: Celebrity Stylist

Rachel Zoe is a celebrity stylist. She has worked with Keira Knightley, Jennifer Garner, and Cameron Diaz. In her book, *Style: A to Zoe*, she explains that after graduating college she went to New York City to become a fashion editor for a magazine. Then she realized she could be dressing stars instead. It is hard work, but she loves it. "The days are [very] long, and it is increasingly normal for me to go three weeks without a day (or night) off," she writes.

Your Fashion Sense

A fashion career might lead to a job as a buyer for a department store. You might work for a business that supports retail stores. Or you might start your own business. Fashion merchandising, marketing, and buying all come into play when you work in a small shop. Over the years, you may gain experience in all those jobs.

CHAPTER 5

DESIGNS ON YOU

Fashion is changing all the time. One of the latest trends is making designer goods more affordable for more people. Vera Wang, for example, is a women's designer who once dressed only rich people. Now she also makes clothes that are sold at Kohl's, a retail department store. Wang's **mass-market** line is called *Simply Vera*. It includes everything from clothing and shoes to home linens and costume jewelry.

Not so long ago, designer looks were hard to find. Only the rich were able to afford designer clothing. Now that more designer fashions are being mass-produced (machine made in large quantities), higher quality merchandise is available for everyone. Discount stores such as Target now sell items from famous designers including Isaac Mizrahi, Todd Oldham, and Michael Graves. Suddenly fashion buying has become even more interesting.

Fashion Types

Haute couture refers to the creation of high, cutting-edge, one-of-a-kind fashions. That means fashion

Well-known fashion designer Vera Wang made a name for herself selling wedding gowns. Today her brand includes clothing, housewares, and more.

30 D
Sun

5
12
19
2%

that few people can have or afford. High fashion is an exciting part of the industry.

Ready-to-wear and mass-market fashions make up the larger part of the business, however.

Large retailers such as The Gap offer a variety of clothing made by machine.

Designers create ready-to-wear clothing in limited quantities and specific sizes. Ready-to-wear clothes are made of fine fabrics. They are usually found only in designer showrooms and boutiques. Mass-market fashions are made by machine. They are produced by the largest manufacturers and can be purchased in retail chain stores and in malls across the United States.

Today, people like to see quality designs in everyday clothing. Images and information travel around the world in an instant — on TV, over cell phones, and on the Internet. New fashion trends spread quickly.

High-Tech Fashion

Like most businesses, fashion moves faster than it once did. Designers used to hand-draw all the pictures of their ideas. Now computer software does much of the work. Software also lets buyers and others see fashion trends as they are happening.

Cash registers in stores are connected to computers that track purchases. Buyers know exactly what items sold in which stores. People in the fashion world use computers at every level of the industry.

Designers on the hit reality TV show *Project Runway* hope to make a name for themselves in the fashion industry.

Ready to Buy?

How does the job of a buyer sound to you? To see whether the fashion world is where you belong, start by working as a sales clerk. You can see what styles customers like and how fashion trends come and go.

When it's time to think about college, consider schools that have fashion programs. They may

Shoe Shopping

A running coach in Oregon put rubber on a waffle iron. Why? He was trying to make shoe bottoms. That experiment was the start of Nike, one of the most successful shoe companies. Companies like Nike do well by doing things differently. Now, Nike and others are leading the way in another trend: allowing customers to design their own sneakers. Converse and Keds do it. Dr. Martens, the bootmaker, had a contest for it. How might this affect fashion trends?

offer two- and four-year degrees. Fashion students can sometimes apply for internships. Students report to stores and work with people who have experience. Many department stores have special training programs for would-be buyers.

Fashion is an ever-changing business. If you are willing to work hard, making fashion your business may just be a stylish career for you!

FASHION BUYER

OUTLOOK

- The United States had 157,000 wholesale and retail fashion buyers in 2006.
- Retail buyers are about 11 percent of all buyers.

WHAT YOU'LL DO

- Fashion buyers keep track of the number of goods in a store. They keep tabs on sale levels. They also read magazines and trade news to see what their competitors are doing. It is a buyer's job to be aware of trends.
- Fashion buyers who work for large firms often track just a few lines of merchandise. Buyers who work for small businesses usually select all items for the store.

WHAT YOU'LL NEED

- Earning a bachelor's degree in a related field, such as business, puts buyers at an advantage. These jobs sometimes offer on-the-job training.
- Retail firms prefer employees who have graduated college. Many retail firms recruit college grads and train them. Employees usually begin as salespeople.

WHAT YOU'LL EARN

- Fashion buyers in wholesale and retail earn between $26,270 and $83,080.
- Retail buyers may also get cash bonuses based on their performance.

Source: U.S. Department of Labor, Bureau of Labor Statistics

GLOSSARY

accessories — articles of dress that complete outfits, such as handbags, belts, and hats

advertising — describes announcements that sell things

budget — a specific amount of money available for a purpose

collaboration — act of working together

consultants — people who help clients with ideas or by giving advice

designers — people who decide how things will look and be constructed

haute couture — high fashion; the most expensive level of the fashion industry, often involving one-of-a-kind designs

internship — a low-level position that helps a person train for a job

marketers — people who promote brands and clothing lines to fashion buyers, consumers, and media professionals, such as magazine editors

mass market — describes machine-sewn clothing that is made in large quantities and sold in retail stores

merchandising — planning, promoting, and selling goods and clothing and helping retail stores create appealing displays

ready-to-wear — describes clothing made by designers in limited quantities and ready-made sizes that often use fine fabrics

retail — describes goods that are sold directly to the public

showrooms — places where designers show off their designs

suppliers — people who provide materials to make goods

trade exhibitions — large displays of objects to the general public or to special audiences by businesses that produce similar goods

trends — current styles that are popular

wholesale — describes goods that are sold in large amounts to buyers that will be sold again to the public

TO FIND OUT MORE

Books

Fashion History: Looking Great Through the Ages. World of Fashion (series). Jen Jones (Capstone Press, 2007)

Fashion Trends: How Popular Style Is Shaped. World of Fashion (series). Jen Jones. (Capstone Press, 2007)

Passion for Fashion. Jeanne Beker. (Tundra Books, 2008)

Working in the Fashion Industry. My Future Career (series). Margaret McAlpine (Gareth Stevens, 2005)

Web Sites

American Apparel and Footwear Association

www.apparelandfootwear.org

Take a peek at the serious side of fashion. Read about ways the industry is trying to make the world a better place.

ArtSchools.com

www.artschools.com/articles/fashion/intro.html

Check out fashion schools across the country to find those that interest you.

***Elle* Girl**

ellegirl.elle.com

Read about current fashion, take *Elle* quizzes, play games like "Rock the Runway," and more.

Seventeen

www.seventeen.com/fashion

Explore all kinds of fashionable fun. Watch *Seventeen* TV, a video link that shows what people are wearing on the streets.

INDEX

About the Author

Jessica Cohn lives in Westchester County, New York, where she runs a publishing firm. She especially enjoys researching interesting topics and thinking about new ideas. Jessica has written books about many kinds of jobs, from aerospace workers to vocational teachers. Every job is interesting, she says, when you look at it closely!